W9-AMN-786

A New True Book

SUBMARINES

By David Petersen

CHILDRENS PRESS ™

CHICAGO

Insignia patches of various U.S. submarines

PHOTO CREDITS

Joseph A. DiChello, Jr.—2, 39

©Ray F. Hillstrom—4

Naval Photographic Center, Washington, D.C.—Cover, 6, 16, 20, 22, 23 (left), 24, 41, 42, 44

Historical Pictures Service, Inc., Chicago, Illinois—9, 11, 13, 18

U.S. Naval Institute Photo Collection—14 (left)

U.S. Naval Historical Center—14 (right)

DAVA Still Media Depository, Washington, D.C.—23 (right), 25, 31, 32, 3; 37

©Wayne A. Bladholm—27

Woods Hole Oceanographic Institution, Woods Hole, MA—28

COVER—U.S.S. Ohio

Library of Congress Cataloging in Publication Data

Petersen, David.
    Submarines.

    (A New true book)
    Includes index.
    Summary: Presents a history of underwater boats, and describes various kinds of submarines, their parts, and personnel.
    1. Submarine boats—Juvenile literature. [1. Submarines] I. Title. II. Series.
V857.P48   1984   359.3'257   83-26253
ISBN 0-516-01728-4   AACR2

TABLE OF CONTENTS

U.S.S. *Silversides,* a retired World War II submarine berthed in Chicago, Illinois

WHAT IS A SUBMARINE?

The word *submarine* comes from two other words: *sub,* which means "under," and *marine,* which means "water."

So, *submarine* means "underwater." And that's a good name, because submarines are designed to sail underwater.

Submarines can dive hundreds or even thousands of feet deep. They can stay

Above: U.S.S. *Seafox*
Above right: U.S.S. *Tigrone*
Right: U.S.S. *Greyback*

underwater for long periods
of time, moving about as
they please.

Some other names for
submarine are sub, U-boat,
and DSV.

Sub is an abbreviation for submarine. U-boat stands for underwater boat.

DSV stands for Deep Submergence Vehicle. DSVs are often designed for scientific exploration and study of the deepest parts of the world's oceans.

Bell-shaped DSVs are called diving bells. Egg-shaped DSVs are called bathyscaphes.

A MAN WITH A VISION

In 1869, a Frenchman with a good imagination about the future wrote a book called *Twenty Thousand Leagues Under the Sea*. It was about a boat that was able to travel underwater for great distances without having to come up for air or fuel.

The French writer's name was Jules Verne, and his imaginary underwater boat

An artist's drawing of the *Nautilus* (left) and his idea of what the view might have been from a window of the *Nautilus* (above)

was named the *Nautilus*. (A nautilus is a sea creature that lives on the bottom of the ocean in a shell.)

When Jules Verne wrote his book, people thought that an underwater boat could never be built.

How could anyone ever invent a boat that could dive as deep, stay under as long, and travel as far and fast as the *Nautilus*? But those people were wrong.

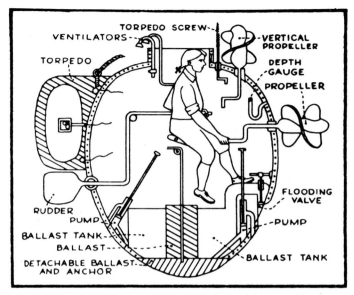

A diagram of
the *Turtle*

THE HISTORY OF

UNDERWATER BOATS

One of the earliest
underwater boats, the *Turtle*,
was built in America. The
Turtle looked like a big
wooden egg. It carried one
man, who turned a

handcrank to drive a propeller that slowly pushed the boat along. In 1776, during the revolutionary war between America and Britain, the *Turtle* was used to attack the British warship *Eagle.*

The attack took place in New York Harbor. The *Turtle* did not sink the *Eagle*, but being attacked by an underwater boat did scare the British ship away.

One of the first submarines designed for

An illustration of the *Argonaut* on a wrecking expedition

scientific exploration of the
oceans was made in 1897
and called the *Argonaut*.
This egg-shaped sub had
wheels like a car, so it
could roll along the bottom
of the ocean. But the
wheels didn't work very

13

well, since they would get stuck in the deep sand and mud on the ocean's floor.

The first U.S. Navy submarine was launched in 1900 and named the U.S.S. *Holland*. "U.S.S." stands for United States ship.

Left: John P. Holland in the conning tower of the U.S.S. *Holland*
Below: U.S.S. *Holland* out of the water for repairs, photographed in 1900

During World War I, between 1914 and 1918, Germany made many very important improvements in submarines. German submarines of that time were called U-boats. They were used for war.

These German U-boats fired underwater bombs called torpedoes. Torpedoes have their own propellers, and can travel very fast after they are fired from a submarine.

15

The German submarine, U-3008, photographed in 1947

In 1914, near the coast of Scotland, a German submarine named *U-21* used torpedoes to sink the British battle cruiser *Pathfinder*. This was the first ship ever sunk by a torpedo fired from a submarine.

After that, submarines became more and more important in naval warfare.

In May of 1915, a German U-boat torpedoed a British passenger ship named the H.M.S. (His Majesty's Ship) *Lusitania*. Over a thousand civilians were aboard the *Lusitania*, and most of them died.

Many of the people who died on the *Lusitania* were Americans. The sinking of the *Lusitania* was one of

The sinking of the *Lusitania*

the reasons that the United
States decided to declare
war on Germany in 1917.

The United States had
submarines in World War I,
too. The men who sailed on
them called them "pig
boats" because they were

so small, and there wasn't
enough water for everyone
to keep clean.

By the end of World War I,
in 1918, three countries had
military submarines:
America, Britain (England),
and Germany.

Submarines were used by
the navies of many
countries during World War II
(1939 to 1945). During
these years submarines
became bigger, faster, more
comfortable, and safer.

But the most important change in submarines wouldn't come until the 1950s. It was an improvement so great that all other submarines that had been built before would soon come to be considered useless antiques.

U.S.S. *Sailfish* in 1945

ATOMIC SUBMARINES

In 1954 for the first time atomic power was used to propel submarines. Atomic power is called "nuclear power." The *Nautilus*, the world's first nuclear-powered submarine, was launched by the United States Navy.

The U.S.S. *Nautilus* was named after the submarine in *Twenty Thousand Leagues Under the Sea.*

The nuclear-powered submarine U.S.S. *Nautilus* in a rough sea

But the modern *Nautilus* could do even more things than Jules Verne's imaginary underwater boat could. It was the first submarine to sail under the ice at the North Pole.

Above: The watch crew of the U.S.S. *Nautilus*
maintains exact course and depth as
the submarine passes under the Polar ice cap.
Right: A crew member performs a routine check
on the torpedo tubes of the U.S.S. *Nautilus.*

By sailing under the ice, called the Polar ice cap, the *Nautilus* was able to go directly from the Pacific Ocean to the Atlantic Ocean.

Later, nuclear submarines would learn how to surface

U.S.S. *Triton*

through the thick ice of the Polar caps.

In 1960, another American nuclear sub, the U.S.S. *Triton*, sailed completely around the world— underwater!

In that same year, 1960, the British launched their first nuclear-powered sub, the H.M.S. *Dreadnaught.*

The newest and biggest nuclear submarine in the world is named the U.S.S. *Ohio.* The *Ohio* is 560 feet

U.S.S. *Ohio*

long, and cost $1.2 *billion* to build! The *Ohio* was launched in November, 1982. It carries twenty-four missiles that can be fired while the sub is submerged.

Today, four countries have nuclear submarines: America, Britain, the USSR (Russia), and France.

Sea Link I, owned by Johnson and Johnson, is a research vessel that can operate at a depth of 1500 feet. It is battery powered and can operate underwater for more than six hours. It has underwater photographic and video equipment and robot arms that can be used to pick up marine samples. *Sea Link I* is leased with a crew to research groups throughout the world.

SCIENTIFIC EXPLORATION SUBMARINES

Deep Submergence Vehicles, or DSVs for short, are designed to do scientific research and exploration in the deepest parts of the deepest oceans of the world.

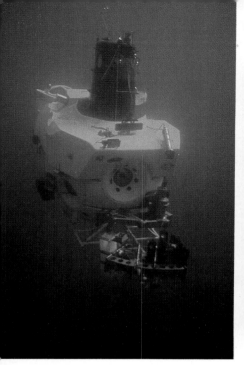
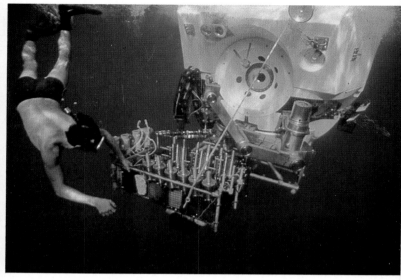

Two views of the DSV *Alvin* underwater

The most famous of all DSVs is named *Alvin*. *Alvin* is based at the Woods Hole Oceanographic Institution in Massachusetts.

Alvin was built in 1964. It can carry three men and stay on the bottom of the ocean for up to eight hours. After that, it runs out of air for the crew to breathe, and must surface.

Alvin was the first submarine to dive over one mile deep. That's 5,280 feet under the water!

At a mile deep, there is no light, and the water is cold and black. *Alvin* makes about one hundred dives each year. *Alvin* has made many important discoveries about the ocean and the kinds of animals and plants that live in its deepest places.

But there are other DSVs that can dive even deeper than *Alvin*.

In 1960, the DSV *Trieste* took two men down to 35,800 feet! That was in one of the deepest places in the ocean, called the Mariana Trench, near the little island of Guam, in the Pacific.

Some submarines are owned by private companies. Businesses use

their subs to search for
sunken treasure that has
been lying on the bottom of
the ocean for hundreds of
years. Sometimes, DSVs can
bring up all or parts of
sunken ships and airplanes.

An underwater view of a Deep Submergence Rescue Vehicle (DSRV 1)

The *Sealab III Habitat* is used for experiments in underwater living by scientists

Other bathyscaphes are designed to rescue sailors from sunken submarines that are stranded hundreds of feet underwater. These subs are called Deep Submergence Rescue Vehicles, or DSRVs.

Japan has a small submarine named the *Aquamarine*. It holds four passengers, and is used for underwater farming and fishing.

Many scientists who study the oceans believe that underwater farming will become very important. Someday, there will be too many people in the world for regular farmers to feed. Then, we'll have to start growing foods underwater.

With the *Aquamarine*, Japan is already doing this!

MIDGET SUBMARINES

Even though subs cost thousands of dollars, some people own their own submarines! These "family subs" are usually very small, and will carry only one or two people at a time.

Small submarines are called midget subs, or mini-subs. Most people who own mini-subs use them for pleasure. They like to float around hundreds of feet underwater to look at the fish and other ocean life.

One man in Geneva, Switzerland, carries passengers in his submarine.

This sub, named the *Auguste Piccard* after its owner, has made more than 850 dives and has taken more than 25,000 people for underwater rides!

If you're ever in Switzerland, maybe *you* might get to ride in the *Auguste Piccard!*

Crewmen in the control room of the nuclear-powered U.S.S. *Ohio*

PEOPLE WHO WORK ON SUBMARINES

The people who live and work on submarines are called the crew. There are many jobs that the crew must do on a submarine as big as the *Nautilus* or the U.S.S. *Ohio*.

The captain is in charge of everything. He gives the orders, and makes all the important decisions.

There are also people whose jobs are to steer the sub and to operate its many complicated radios and electronic equipment. Others take care of the big nuclear reactors that make the power to propel the sub through the water.

And there are many more jobs, too, including radar and sonar operators, and

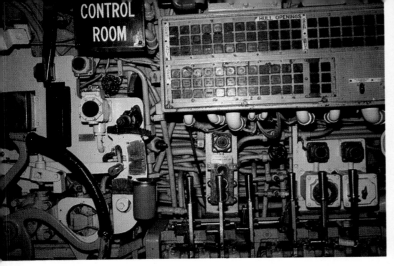

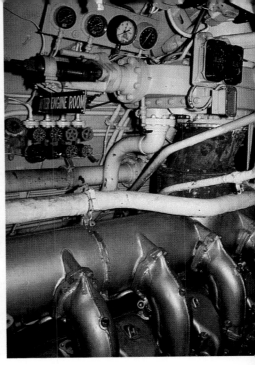

These interior shots were taken in the U.S.S. *Croaker*, a retired U.S. submarine berthed in Groton, Connecticut.
Above left: The control room
Bottom left: The galley and mess hall
Above: The after engine room

even doctors and cooks. A big submarine will have a crew of over one hundred people!

IMPORTANT PARTS OF A SUBMARINE

The outside shell of a submarine is called the hull. The hull is thick steel. It protects the people and equipment inside from the great pressures of the deep oceans.

The sail is the part that sticks up above the hull of a nuclear sub. The sail is where the captain guides the sub when it is sailing on top of the water.

You can clearly see the sail of the U.S.S. *Ohio*.

In older, non-nuclear submarines, the sail was called the conning tower.

The nuclear reactor is the heart of an atomic submarine. The reactor produces so much heat that seawater will boil and turn

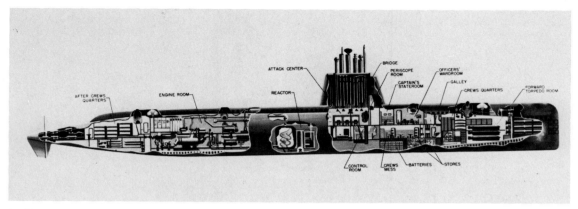

A diagram of the U.S.S. *Nautilus*

to steam. The steam wants
to escape, and is forced to
pass through huge turbines.
The turbines turn very fast,
and power the propellers
that push the sub along.

Nuclear submarines can
travel thirty miles an hour
underwater. That is faster
than most ships and boats
can go on the surface!

One of the most important parts of a submarine is the periscope. A periscope is a hollow tube that sticks up above the water like an eye.

A periscope has mirrors and lenses that allow people in a submerged submarine to see above the top of the water. With a periscope, the captain of a submarine can watch ships on the surface of the ocean,

U.S.S. *Triton* underway

without those ships being able to see the submarine.

All military submarines have periscopes, even the most modern nuclear-powered models.

SUBMARINES: YESTERDAY, TODAY, AND TOMORROW

Many years ago, people thought that they would always be creatures of the land, and would never be able to travel in the air, in space, or underwater.

But today, there are rockets that can take people to the moon. And there are nuclear submarines that can travel completely around the world underwater!

Science is wonderful.

WORDS YOU SHOULD KNOW

bathyscaphe(BATH • ih • skaf)—a term applied to early Deep Submergence Vehicles

boat(BOTE)—a small seagoing vessel (as the term is used by navies). All submarines prior to nuclear submarines were classified as boats.

conning tower(KAHN • ing TOW • er)—the boxlike structure rising from the deck of a submarine, used for observation and steering when surfaced. On nuclear submarines, the conning tower is called a "sail."

deck(DEHK)—a floor or walking area on a ship or boat

dive(DYVE)—the term used when a submarine submerges

knot(NOT)—a measurement of speed for ships and boats, equal to one nautical mile per hour

league(LEEG)—a unit of measure used by ships and boats, and equal to three nautical miles

marine(mah • REEN)—having to do with the ocean: marine life, marine biology, submarine, etc.

mariner(MARE • in • er)—a sailor

nautical mile(NAW • tih • kil MYLE)—an international unit of measure used by ships, boats, and airplanes, and equal to 1,852 meters, or 6,076 feet (a little over a mile)

nuclear powered(NOO • klee • er POW • ird)—using atomic power to heat water that drives steam turbines that turn the propellers that drive a ship

oceanography(OH • shin • OG • ra • fee)—the scientific study of the ocean

periscope(PAIR • ih • skope)—a hollow tube fitted with a series of mirrors that allows the crew of a submerged submarine to see the surface

porthole(PORT • hohl)—an opening in a ship's side to admit light or air, and usually protected by glass

sail(SAYLE)—on nuclear submarines, a structure on the top deck used for observation and surface steering. On nonnuclear submarines, this same structure is called the "conning tower."

ship—any large, seagoing sailing craft. Nuclear submarines are called ships, while older, smaller submarines were known as boats.

sonar(SOH • nar)—an electronic device that sends out underwater sound waves, then records their echoes on a screen. Sonar is used for navigation by submerged submarines.

submarine(SUB • mah • reen)—underwater. Anything that lives, moves, or is underwater. A submarine is an underwater boat or ship.

submerge(sub • MIRJ)—to go underwater; same as dive, in submarine terminology

submersibles(sub • MER • sih • bils)—diving vessels intended for deep submergence, and not as mobile as submarines, as in bathyscaphes, diving bells, and DSVs or Deep Submergence Vehicles

tender(TEN • der)—a class of ships that follow and supply other ships, as in submarine tender

torpedo(tor • PEA • doh)—a bomb-shaped cylinder that is self-propelled and fired from a submarine at another ship or boat

INDEX

About the author

David Petersen has been a Marine Corps aviator, a magazine editor, a college teacher, and a free-lance writer, editor, and photographer. He is currently an associate editor for The Mother Earth News, *in Hendersonville, North Carolina.* Submarines *is his fifth True Book.*